Jayden Gains Confidence

Lourdine Joseph

Illustrated by Sanaa

Copyright © 2022 Lourdine Joseph

All rights reserved. This book should not be reproduced or transmitted in any form, printed or digital, without the consent of the author.

Jayden was feeling very excited as he walked home from school. It was the beginning of summer vacation and he had so many things that he wanted to do during the vacation. He planned to go camping with his friends and play at the pool! His friends Ryan and John had suggested that they should visit the Blue Lagoon! Jayden happily smiled to himself when he thought about it. Things were looking good!

Just then, he heard a voice from behind him.

"Hey there, small man with big ears!"

Jayden felt his ears turning red. He hated the fact that his ears were a little bigger than what suited his face. Still, was it a reason for his classmates to make jokes? Jayden's good mood vanished immediately. He felt himself becoming gloomy.

The other kids kept calling him names, and soon, Jayden's gloomy mood turned into anger. He turned around to yell at the mean kids. But before he could do anything, Ryan and John came running.

"Sorry we are late!" said Ryan, "Mrs. Rolle wanted to talk to us about something..." Jayden watched the mean kids slowly backing away. Soon, they were all gone.

"Why do you look upset?" John wanted to know.

"It's nothing..." said Jayden, "Let's just go home."

Jayden was glad that the vacation was starting. It meant that he could get away from the mean kids for some time. He was glad that he had Ryan and John on his side no matter what.

After going home, Jayden told his mom about what happened to him. Jayden loved his mom and dad very much. They loved him a lot and got him everything he needed to be happy.

Whenever Jayden was upset and tearful about being bullied, his mom always consoled him.

She did her best to make Jayden feel better.

"You are amazing and wonderfully made," she told Jayden as she hugged him, "You must learn how to appreciate yourself and be happy. You are a kind, caring, and talented boy. You're very smart too. I am so proud of you! One day, others would see just how awesome you are!"

"Thanks, mom!" Jayden said. But he was still skeptical about what his mom said. If he was so awesome, why were others taking him for a joke? While Jayden was wallowing in sorrow, his mom took him to fish fry for conch salad and fritters to cheer him up. It helped a little and he was grateful to her.

As time passed, Jayden forgot about all the bad memories he had accumulated at school. His vacation mode was in full swing! He got to play with his two best friends and do all sorts of fun summer activities.

One day, Jayden, Ryan, and John went swimming in the pool. Jayden was a very talented swimmer. Sometimes, his dad joked that he was half dolphin! The three friends held a friendly swimming competition, and Jayden won quite easily.

"Whoo-hoo!" he yelled happily as he did a somersault underwater, "I won!"

"You are such a great swimmer," Ryan said, "Perhaps you are a dolphin hybrid like your dad says!"

"I want a rematch!" John said, "This time, I will win!"

And so, they started swimming again. Jayden won the second round as well. He got out of the pool and waited with a grin for his friends to finish.

"Alright, alright…" said John as he got out of the pool, "You are the champion!" "I am!" Jayden said with a laugh.

"I am SOOOOOO sad!" John said, pretending to cry. Everyone knew that he was just joking, but Jayden decided to play along with him.

"Don't be sad," he said, "Do you want me to buy you a juice box?" "Yes, please!" said John, beaming.

"You were aiming for that all along!" laughed Ryan.

And so, they went to the cafeteria at the pool after changing. Jayden bought juice boxes for all three.

While Ryan and John were walking away with their juice boxes, a mean boy named Sam started joking about Jayden's ears. He was a boy from their class.

"You have monkey ears!" Sam laughed.

It made Jayden very angry. He wanted to get into a fight with Sam.

"Take that back!" yelled Jayden.

Hearing Jayden yelling angrily, Ryan and John looked back to check what was going on.

Jayden was about to punch Sam when Ryan and John stopped him.

"You don't have to do that Jayden," Ryan said.

"He insulted me, and said I have monkey ears…" Jayden replied.

"Is that true Sam?" asked Ryan, "That's very immature of you. You should apologize!"

Sometimes, Ryan acted very maturely. He knew exactly how to resolve conflicts between his friends.

Sam shrugged in response to Ryan's remark. He was very playful and always got himself into trouble. He was very arrogant and never listened to anyone. So, when Ryan asked him to apologize to Jayden, he refused.

"You don't have to be like this," Ryan said, "Everyone is unique and perfect. No one can be like you, and no one can be like Jayden."

"Why can't you apologize?" John asked Sam, "Don't you know that jokes like that can make people feel hurt?"

Sam took a deep breath and apologized.

"I am sorry, Jayden," Sam said. He looked genuinely sorry.

Jayden hugged him and said, "I am also sorry for trying to hit you."

John and Ryan appreciated Sam for apologizing. Jayden thanked Ryan for being so brave and mature in handling the situation. Later, they all went back to Ryan's house to play a new video game. It made Jayden cheer up to a certain extent.

Jayden told his mom about what happened with Sam. He also told her how Ryan had helped solve the problem. Jayden's mom called Ryan to thank him for helping and defending her son.

"Sometimes, others make fun of you," Jayden's mom told him, "It can happen to anyone. You have to learn how to resolve those conflicts and move on without getting emotionally hurt."

"I know, mom…" said Jayden, "But they make me so angry!"

"You can't win a conflict by fighting or throwing stones at each other," his mom explained,

"That will only make things worse. You must win by wisdom…"

"I understand now, mom," Jayden replied.

"I want you to be a good child, and I know you are already," Mom patted his back, "When other kids make fun of you at school, you must not take their jokes to heart. You should focus on your studies rather than getting upset by their comments. That will show everyone that you are not one to joke about. I know that you will make all of us proud."

Her words made Jayden feel a lot better. He forgot about all his worries and focused on having fun during the vacation. He got to do so many fun activities with Ryan and John. They went swimming with the pigs in the beautiful waters of Exuma, visited the pink sand beaches in Eleuthera, and they even swam with the dolphins. It was the best summer Jayden had ever had.

He wished the holidays would never end.

However, all good things must come to an end. Finally, the summer vacation was over, and it was time to go back to school again.

Jayden's mom bought him a new bag, shoes, and a flask. But Jayden was not happy about going to school because he felt that his classmates would make fun of him again. Although he wished that the holidays would never end, he knew that it was not a realistic wish. Now that the holidays were over, it was time for him to go back to school.

The first few days after the vacation were a little difficul[t]. He kept wishing that it was still summer vacation. One d[ay] a note on his desk which had a sketch of a kid with big [ears] in the sketch was flying in the sky by flapping his hu[ge ears.] drawing brought tears to Jayden's eyes. He tore up th[e note and] threw it out of the window. He could hear his classmates snickering in the background. He took a deep breath and pretended that he could not hear them. After some time, the whispering and snickering sounds faded away.

"Mom was right," Jayden thought, "There is no point in reacting to these taunts. I have to focus on my studies."

The mean kids still called him names, but Jayden reminded himself that he was special, unique, and talented. He still got angry at their jokes as it was natural to be angry at insults.

But instead of lashing out, Jayden focused all his extra energy on studying.

One day, Mrs. Rolle gave everyone an assignment to complete within an hour. She promised them a present if they did well. A lot of kids were worried because they had not studied. But Jayden felt confident because he knew that he would do well. When the time was up, Mrs. Rolle asked them to submit their work. Jayden scored the highest, and his classmate Aaliyah came second.

"You're awesome, Jayden!" whispered Ryan and John.

Mrs. Rolle called Aaliyah to the front of the class and gave her some storybooks, asking her to share them with Jayden.

But Aaliyah took all the books for herself without giving Jayden any

of them. Jayden waited some time for her to share the books with him. But when she did not, he decided to ask about it.

"Mrs. Rolle gave them to me," said Aaliyah, "So, I'm keeping them."

Jayden felt himself becoming angry. How could Aaliyah be so unfair?! But instead of arguing with her, Jayden decided to tell Mrs. Rolle about it. He knew that it was the best way to resolve the conflict. Like his mom and Ryan always said, fighting and arguing never solved anything.

So, Jayden reported to Mrs. Rolle about what Aaliyah had done. Mrs. Rolle asked Aaliyah to come forward. She collected the books from Aaliyah and asked her to face the class and apologize.

"You shouldn't be greedy, Aaliyah…" Mrs. Rolle said, "Now apologize to Jayden and the rest of the class."

"I'm sorry for acting so selfish, Jayden…" said Aaliyah.

"It's alright," said Jayden, "Everyone makes mistakes. What matters is that we learn from them."

After going home that day, Jayden told his mom what had happened. His mom was happy that he reported the case to the teacher without fighting with Aaliyah.

"You're growing up to be a very sensible young man," said his mom, "You will always make us proud."

As days passed, Jayden found out that he was no longer bothered about the jokes others were making about him. He still felt upset, but he knew that pondering over it would only make him feel worse. He found solace in studying and did well in all his classes. Thanks to his studying, Jayden did well in his examinations. Soon, the examination was over, and the results were out. Jayden's mom received results from the school. Jayden was the best student in his class! His parents were very proud of him.

"I knew you could do it, Jayden!" said his mom, "You overcame all the obstacles in your way. You made us all proud!"

Jayden felt very proud of his achievement too. Although the kids in his school had called him names and made fun of him, he had managed to overcome all of that.

Jayden was even more excited to hear from Mrs. Rolle that he would be awarded a prize for performing so well in his exams. John and Ryan were also happy for him. They knew how much Jayden had been mocked in the school. Ryan could remember when Jayden was called a "short man with big ears". Despite everything, Jayden had managed to do well. He was an inspiration to everyone.

Some of Jayden's classmates apologized to him for calling him names. Jayden forgave them and told them never to mock anyone else like that. He knew he always had the support of Ryan and Jayden behind him so, he was not much affected by the insults. Jayden knew that he was building up his self-esteem and confidence step by step. He needed to be able to stand on his own, even without the help of his friends. And he felt that he was getting there slowly yet surely.

On the day of the award ceremony, Jayden's mom went to school to attend the award ceremony. Jayden was a little sad that his dad could not make it since he had a busy day at work.

At the ceremony, the senior mistress asked Jayden to come to the stage and everyone applauded. Jayden smiled and walked to the front. Mom, Ryan, and John waved at him.

While Jayden walked up to the stage, he could hear the familiar insults in his mind, "big ears, short man." But Jayden knew that it was all in his head.

"I am confident of myself," he told the voices in his head, "This award ceremony is a symbol of me overcoming my trauma of being bullied."

And soon, the voices in his head became quiet. Jayden walked to the center of the stage with confidence and stood in front of all the students. It was an overwhelming feeling, but he felt victorious.

The senior mistress congratulated Jayden and presented him with an award.

"You're an amazing student, Jayden!" she said, "Your results have improved so much from your last exams. Would you like to tell your fellow students about it?"

Jayden took the microphone from the senior mistress. He was feeling a little nervous. But he had some things that he needed to tell the other kids.

"Good day to you all," he said, "You all probably know me as the small man with big ears."

At his words, some students looked confused, a few of them laughed, and some others looked at the floor with guilty eyes.

"I was often mocked because of my big ears," Jayden said, "But my parents and my best friends, Ryan and John, were always there for me. They helped me see that I was special and unique. I am perfect the way I am. Insults and mockery would never push me down. I am here today as a result of me taking it upon myself to overcome bullying. And I would like to thank everyone who helped me."

Ryan and John started clapping and cheering. Jayden saw his mom wiping away a tear of happiness. Soon, the other students were applauding too. Jayden felt that they were applauding him not only because he did well in exams, but also because he managed to overcome bullying.

"You are an inspiration to everyone, Jayden," said the senior mistress. Then, she turned to face the audience. "I hope that all of you learned something from Jayden. Now, we have to commence school activities. So, all of you can go back to your classes."

And so, everyone went to their classes. A lot of kids congratulated Jayden on his achievement. Mrs. Rolle also congratulated him and gave him a present. Jayden felt that it was the best day of his life.

When Jayden got home, he saw that his mom had already prepared his favorite meal. She had also made peas soup and dumpling.

"Thank you, mom!" Jayden said as he hugged his mom.

"I am proud of you, my son." Mom said, touching his cheeks. His dad also came home early to celebrate.

Jayden helped Dad carry his briefcase. When he took it inside, his dad told him to open it.

And when he did, he saw a brand-new video game inside!

"That's my gift to you," dad said with a smile, "Congratulations on becoming the best student, champ!"

Jayden was very happy and excited. He loved the game his dad brought him and he loved the meal his mom had prepared for him. After enjoying the meal together, Jayden's mom also presented him with a gift. It was a book with positive affirmations. Jayden took it to his room, lay down on the bed, and started reading. He found the book to be very interesting.

"Success is for everyone, No one is left out of it. Success is for everyone, No one is left out of it.

Success is for everyone

I will succeed, I will make Mom proud.

I will make Dad proud.

I will make my friends proud.

Success is for everyone."

Jayden felt that the book had been written especially for him. It made him feel special and empowered.

His mom passed by his room and was happy to hear him reciting the affirmations from his book. Jayden could see mom peeking from behind the doors.

"I can see you, mom!" he laughed, "What are you doing there?" Mom came into the room and smiled at him.

"So, do you like the book?" she asked. Jayden nodded in reply.

"I love my body the way it is," Jayden said, "I love myself, mom. Thank you for helping me see how special I am."

Jayden hugged his mom. She was happy that he could affirm those statements.

On the next day at school, Jayden, Ryan, and John made plans to see the Junkanoo parade on Boxing Day and New Year's Day. They were all excited to see all the colorful costumes and listen to the steady beat of whistles, cowbells and goatskin drums on Bay Street.

While they were discussing their plans, some of their classmates came to talk to Jayden. He realized that they were the kids who had called him names in the past. However, they seemed to be nervous about something.

"Can I help you?" asked Jayden.

One of the bullies finally spoke up.

"We are sorry that we called you names, Jayden…" the bully said, "We were so inspired by your story yesterday. Will you forgive us?"

"Of course," Jayden said, "I have put all of that behind me." "I wish I could be like you too…" said another kid.

Jayden thought for a moment. He decided that he could share his affirmations with his classmates.

"Whenever you feel bad about yourself, tell yourself this," Jayden said.

"I love myself. I am unique.

My body is unique.

I am different.

Created for a purpose. To shine forth. I am unique.

I refuse to be intimidated.

I will make everyone happy.

My eyes are beautiful.

My nose is perfect. My ears are perfect.

My ears are perfect. My legs are okay.

I am unique."

The kids listened well to Jayden's affirmations and thanked him for sharing. After the kids were gone, Ryan and John came to talk to Jayden.

"Look at you!" said Ryan, "You have learned to love yourself and now you are teaching others how to do it too."

"You are an inspiration to us all," said John.

Jayden smiled happily. He felt that he had finally overcome all the obstacles and emerged victorious. It was truly a wonderful feeling.

THE END

Made in United States
Orlando, FL
21 June 2022